CW00859618

LOVE NOTES

By

JOHN HODGSON

ISBN: 978-1-329-34036-7

PREFACE:

As life brings love and love makes life one must always find time in life to reflect upon your love. When love can be unpredictable, the unpredictability is what makes love stronger to the one you love. Such love can bring unsurpassed happiness that is always reciprocating and grows ever so sweeter and sweeter. Finding your love is a growing factor of how you view your own love. So, as you read these "Love Notes" think if you will about where you would like to be regarding your own love, if your ready to embark upon your love, are you already in love?, what type of love do you know?, or are you just fooling around? When reading these "Love Notes" you might just find out what your love is all about and what love your lovers love is about. And when you understand this love of your life then you can embark upon a higher love in your life.

KNOWING LOVE

If you get bored, I'll be your guide.
To take you on a grateful ride,
To a life that you show great pride,
Because others will see that your right for me.
And I hope you'll be my soul bride.
I'll make you happy with every word,
'Cause my love is like a bird.
Chirping about with such pride,
About how much I love your stride.
To always love the one that you are,
Even when everything becomes bizarre,
Then our love will be put to the test.
To tell you all the love I confess.
To you; you're the only one I tell.
'Cause I love you even when love is a far.
To make up and find you again,
To love you always is just my plan.
To see my love is to know loves true,
Even when I daze some days seem blue.

John Hodgson

APPLES SING

As an apple falls, another music note is found,
About the lands travelled less far.
Playing the music is just as sweet,
As that apple, apple treat.
Hear the apple red, such as music so divine.
The music is heard, when the apple drops from its
vine. As the apple falls from the vine,
Music is played with such divine.
Grasses grow over the apples,
That are not chosen to hear their peel.
But the music played on, for the apples that did not
get peeled.
'Cause their ears are strong as a gear.
To hear all the songs that is appealed.
So as the apples fall, you must hear,
Their noise and not to be appalled.

LOVE GROWS

As the days play out their fruitfulness,
Love is connected about the lands,
To each and every love plan,
To meet your other half of the day,
First you must always pray,
Then your love doesn't go astray,
But grows about the day and lands,
Playful as a baby lamb,
In time love only grows,
To see everyone in the crowds,
To spot the love that is so proud,
As love is the way it is,
Give love time and you'll find,
That love isn't a waste of time,
But makes life of a living kind,
Love is love and love is life,
If you haven't found your love,
Don't give up because time is of time,
You'll find your right love to last your life,
To spot your love that is perfect as a ball in a glove.

John Hodgson

PLAY LOVE

As people play their loving game,
People love just the same,
Each others named just as plain,
With each and other of their cause,
To enrich their curling love,
With each other, lovers play the cards,
Of each and every note,
And to make a remarkable suite,
Then they feel just so sweet,
With each other of the song,
That is just a revolving cause,
To love each other, even when wrong,
As such love grows so strong,
To last longer than any song,
As each and everyone falls in love,
Trying to love to a higher note,
Always singing a grateful song,
With the love that doesn't go wrong.

GENDER LOVE

If you call on your love,
You know it's true when,
You do what your love knows is true,
And another day that you wish,
For a great day that doen't omit
You from your love and you emit
That you cannot forget the words that other people
say which you pray for the day you meet your love.
'Cause the other day you prayed,
To hear your love of the day,
Then you pray to love another day,
As time is of dismay,
Time travels quickly when love is true,
'Cause you know that love is everywhere,
With your love time is of time,
And your love loves you with little shame,
That you thought, because I love you just the same.

John Hodgson

FIND YOURSELF

To understand what's happening,
You must first love your happy stance,
Know yourself with just a glance,
In the mirror is where you stand,

If and when, just by chance,
You find yourself knowing your stance,
To embark on a mission that you love,
To see yourself just as you are,
Not to pretend yourself too far (away),
From knowing your days that are
Of a new life that is not bizarre,
But is of a presence of yourself,
Not to be mistaken for somebody else,
Love yourself just as you are,
Then you'll find yourself and go far,
In the life where you saw for yourself,
When you where young and not so tall,
To understand what's happening,
You must take your steps so very sharp,
And live a life that you so embark (upon).

TOGETHERNESS

Listen; listen from your heart, each and every remark,
That is made towards your heart,
And you will learn your lovers' smarts,
And have a life that embarks,
Prosperity to each and every remark,
Trusting each other with simple words,
To eventually embark about your worlds,
To trust each others grateful kindness,
That is were success is born,
And love is there to bring the happiness,
You so deserve with all your kindness,
Helping each other to find the love,
That is so great that comes from above,
To reap the rewards that love so brings.

John Hodgson

HEAR THE MUSIC

In the music you hear, the notes that play,
Each and every day, the music plays,
You listen to the notes you choose,
The songs that are to your amuse,
Listen carefully as you choose,
The music that fills your mind,
When you hear the songs that rhyme,
You will learn the greatness of the time,
You spend to hear the music of kind.
When your mind is full of the music,
You will follow the music's grind.
So, make sure of the music and notes you choose,
'Cause music is so amused,
Of you that your mind is like glue,
To the music you so amuse (yourself).

MEET AND GREET

It is easy to forget, forgive and love,
But do not forget where you come from,
'Cause each and everyone you meet,
Will be time spent on your speech,
With what you say, others will say to you
Where are you from?
Answering questions just for fun,
To meet your loving chosen one,
As the questions grow deeper,
You'll find out who you are without your teacher,
Meeting people for your prosperity,
Business as usual, to meet your keeper,
Your opposite will attract the one you love,
Meeting people for all the right reasons,
To develop your truths of Eden,
Such days when people flock,
To find your heart they hope to unlock,
Only to find that your love is for the one,
That you meet with that speech.

John Hodgson

ENJOYING YOU

Energy, energy is given to me,
'Cause our love is so transcending,
Each and every day I praise,
The time with you I do love,
Like a dove I do love,
As time on a clock is so real,
But when I'm with you time stands still,
'Cause I love the way you make me feel,
Our love is genuine like a dove,
Four leave clover I find with love,
'Cause you help me find my love,
Everyday a flower blooms,
Each pedal is of a natures groove,
Feeling good you make me real,
Everyday I tell this to you,
There is no fake in all that's true,
Easy days are full of love,
As needed to entice your love,
'Cause I love the way you make me feel so full,
In my heart of a nature's fuel,
To always love you with all my pull.

CARING (for you)

As time goes by I understand you more and more,
About the times when you glow and glow,
Our indifferences are only thoughts of caring,
About how to learn with each of us sharing,
Our love is as profound as love is so sweet,
With each and every word you say,
I progress my speech with each and every day,
To hear your voice is to hear your spirit,
When I show you just how much I care (for you),
Your voice becomes my music of the chorus,
Songs of love and harmony that I have (for you),
I write my songs on your behalf,
As I hear and speak so much (to you),
Our love isn't blue, but only colours of a love so true.

John Hodgson

CLOUDS THAT MOVE

Over and over the clouds move about the sky,
When I think of your love I feel so high,
High as the clouds above,
Then I see a white dove above,
And it reminds me of our love,
True and pure as the sunlight shines through,
The clouds up above is our love,
Flying a kite to those clouds,
To reach another level of our love,
If our love is proud,
Those clouds will provide a sample,
Of the sunlight that shines so bright,
Though the clouds with all its might,
Then the clouds move about the the sky,
Clearing the way to see only bright sunshine.

12

WHISPER, WHISPER

Whisper, whisper in your ear,
The love that is never fear,
But just truths of my heart in high gear,
The words I say to you,
Are the words you are so very near?
To my heart I trust without fear,
To you I applause my speech,
In which words that are in reach,
To my heart and soul I search my love,
To you I love like a dove,
Upon the world our love will grow,
Like an oyster pearl,
The days I show you how much I love (you),
I wait for the days upon at which you gaze,
In my eyes with the love days,
When our love is true love,
'Cause my love is just a whispering dove.

John Hodgson

ENGAGEMENT

Each and every day I pray,
To meet you at last of games you play,
I'll love you and I hope you'll say,
The same of what I pray everyday,
To be with you on a golden day,
Where the sun shines and people entwine,
About the day at which we play,
Abstract art is where I think,
Where my next day is with you,
Only to see you in a short time,
Praying about the lands of time well spent,
'Cause I think I love you, not to depart,
'Cause my heart cannot depart,
Of when were're alone, I seem to embark,
Upon a love that is so transcendent,
Encouraging each and every part,
Of my love I hope we never depart.

THE END